Is Your Heart Full?

Written by:
Dr. Edith Treviño

COPYRIGHT 2021
dretandcompany.org

DEDICATION:
This book is dedicated to Santiago. My heart is always full because you bring me so much joy.

HELLO!! My name is Dr. ET, and this is my side-kick "Chiquita." We wrote this book for you!! We will share the importance of well-being. Is your heart empty or is it full?

We wrote this book together for you!!

Are you ready?

(YAY!!!)

What is this?

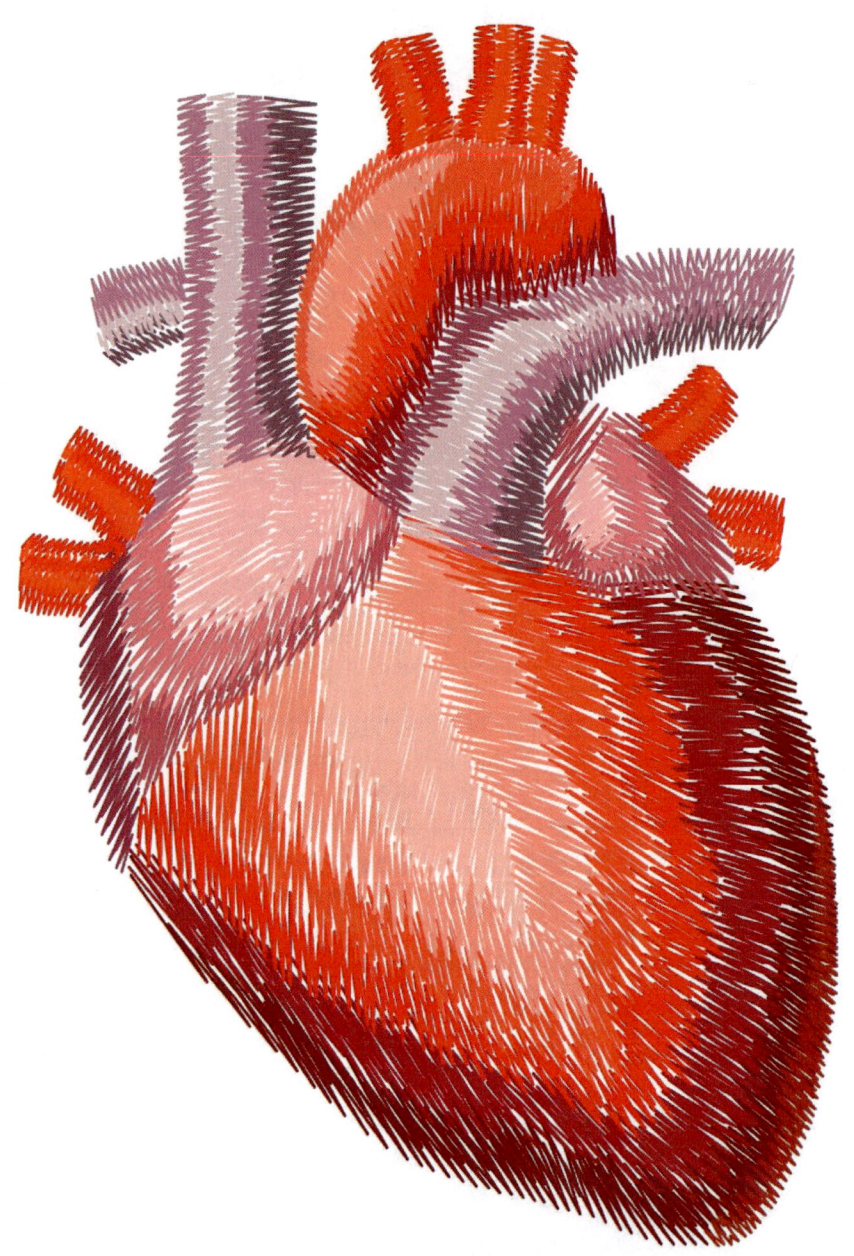

A HEART!

Who has a heart?

We all have a heart.

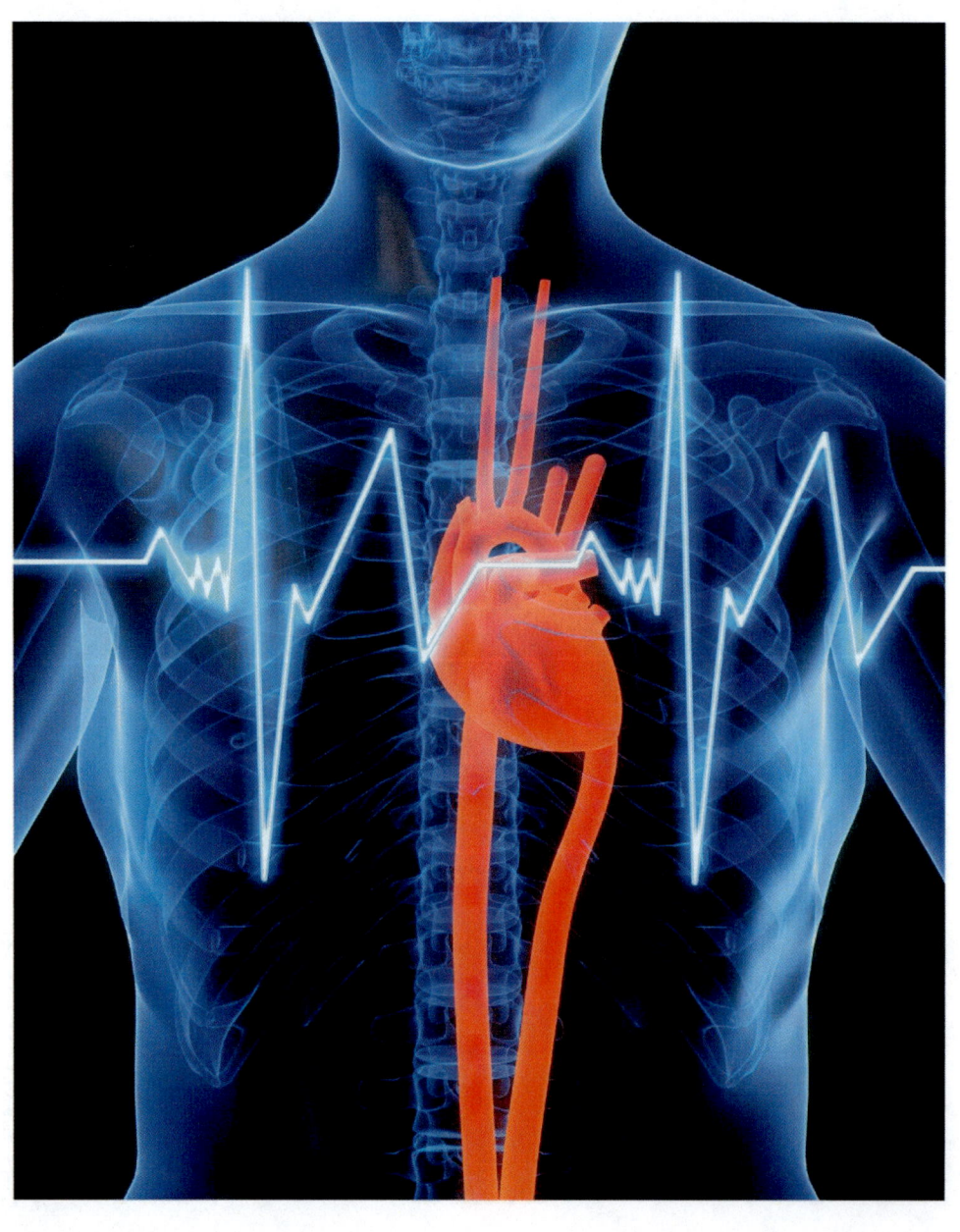

Place your hand on your heart.

What do you hear? What sound does your heart make?
Let's make the sound!

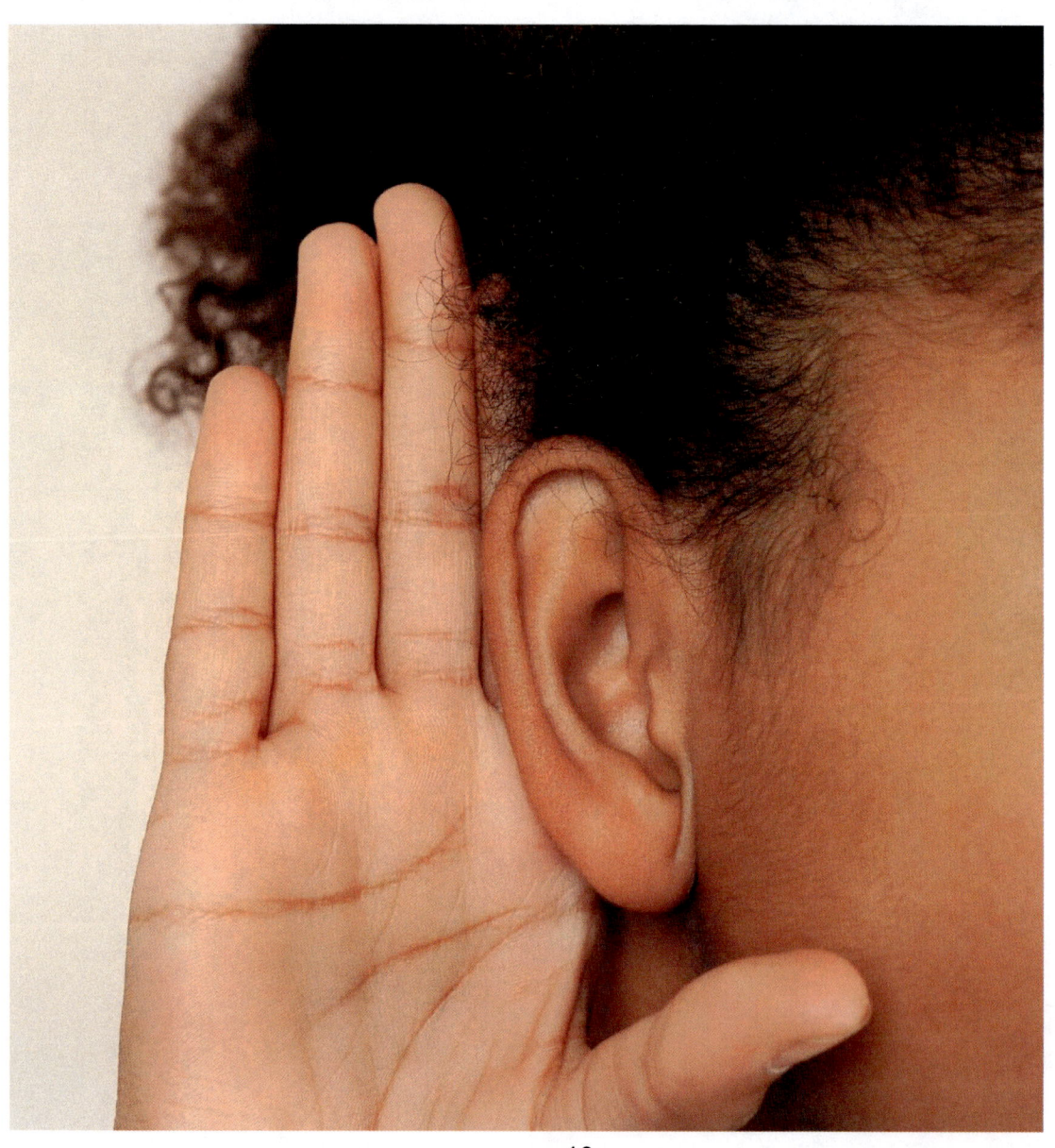

You can also hear your heartbeat with a stethoscope.

What fills your heart with happiness?

1. Being kind to others.
2. Being kind to myself.
3. Respecting others.
4. Respecting myself.
5. Helping others.
6. Being compassionate.
7. Smiling and laughing.
8. Being a good citizen.
9. Caring for others.
10. Being responsible.

What are some examples?

How do you feel when your heart is full?

How does your heart become empty?

How do you feel when your heart is empty?

How can we help refill someone's heart?

What can we do when our hearts are empty?

1. Help someone in need.
2. Smile for 20 seconds.
3. Say kind words to yourself.
4. Ask for help.
5. Be kind.

What are some examples?

Is your heart full, or is your heart empty?

WAYS I PLAN TO FILL MY HEART:

Made in the USA
Middletown, DE
17 August 2023